'Touch of Bouquet

Touch of Bouquet

A CRAFT BOOK
BY TRACY MARSH

Tracy Marsh Publications

Acknowledgement
I would like to thank: little Hannah for her co-operation in modelling the Teddy Bears' Picnic, and
Pam and Terry for the use of their home for the photography.

Also published by Tracy Marsh:
Touch of Nostalgia
Touch of Decor
The Festive Touch
An Introduction to Tole Painting
Touch of Christmas
The Australian Folk Art Collection
Craft & Decorating Magazine

Published by Tracy Marsh Publications
94 Wright Street, Adelaide, South Australia
First published 1986
Second impression January, 1987
Third impression February, 1990
Copyright ©1986 by Tracy Marsh
All rights reserved

ISBN 0 9590174 3 7

Typeset and printed at Griffin Press Limited
Netley, South Australia

Contents

Introduction

My passion for flowers goes back to my childhood days, when I was generally recognised as the neighbourhood flower bandit, scouring the local streets in pursuit of likely floral subjects for pressing, drying, and pot-pourri. That early love of flowers was my inspiration for writing this book.

I derive immense pleasure and relaxation from picking flowers and pressing them, and then waiting with anticipation to see whether they will turn out successfully. Picking your own bouquets of flowers and preserving them to make elegant crafts imparts a quite unique sense of fulfilment and satisfaction. The delights of walking and sitting in a fragrant garden have been treasured since ancient times, and many memorable occasions and festivals have been celebrated with flowers.

The diversity of their delicately haunting fragrances, the beauty of their structure, and their natural grace combine to make flowers a natural choice in the creation of beautiful crafts for gifts and decorations. The simple formula of mixing flowers with a little imagination and a few simple techniques will help you fill the home with colour and fragrance, and bring an immense joy to gift-giving.

I hope that through *Touch of Bouquet* I can share with you my love of re-creating and preserving flowers for interesting craft ideas, and that you will enjoy reading and using the book as much as I have enjoyed creating it.

Tracy Marsh

KNOWING
THE
MATERIALS

Knowing the Materials

You will find it helpful to understand the uses of the different materials and adhesives described below before beginning to make the crafts in this book.

WATER-BASED CRAFT GLUE

A brush can be used for applying a water-based glue. The No. 12 pure-bristle paintbrush is suitable for gluing all types of crafts. The brushes can be cleaned in water after use.

When gluing fabric to pasteboard, coat the pasteboard only—never coat the fabric, as this glue will stain it.

CONTACT ADHESIVE

This type of glue is rubber-based. It is applied with a spatula or finger. It is a very quick-drying fixative, and only small amounts are needed.

SPRAY GLUE

Spray glue is handy when you need to glue large surfaces in the one process. It gives a neat, strong-adhering finish when sprayed on both surfaces.

FABRIC

A variety of different fabrics are used in these crafts. Try to use 100% cotton fabric, and small prints rather than large, bold patterns. Organza, lace fabric, and calico are also used.

STANLEY KNIFE

Suitable for cutting pasteboard and cardboard. Available from hardware shops.

CRAFT KNIFE

Smaller and finer than a Stanley knife, a craft knife is used for cutting the plastic stencils for fabric-painting.

CARDBOARD

There are two types used. One is thick white pasteboard, which can be purchased from art and craft supply shops, or newsagencies. The other is corrugated cardboard, which can be collected from supermarket displays and boxes.

FOAM OR WADDING

10 mm thick foam-sheeting or polyester wadding (used for quilting) are both suitable for padding. Both can easily be stuck with spray glue.

LACES

The increasing popularity of crafts is reflected in the variety of laces available—gathered, straight, torchion, insertion, cotton, and nylon.

RIBBONS

Ribbons are now available in almost every imaginable style and colour. Nylon, satin, polyester, and florist's ribbon are the most frequently used varieties.

POT-POURRI

This sweet-smelling mixture of dried flowers and spices, blended with a fixative, can be used in a wide variety of ways.

POLYESTER FIBREFILL

This fibre padding is used for stuffing cushions and so on. It is available by the bag, from craft and haberdashery shops.

FUSIBLE WEBBING

Also known as 'cobweb', this iron-on material is used to bond two fabrics together. It can be purchased from a haberdashery shop.

FABRIC PAINTS

There are many varieties of fabric paints, some water-based and some acrylic. Brushes used for both types can be cleaned in water. Available from art and craft shops.

THIN PLASTIC SHEETING

Used for fabric-painting, and available from plastic supply outlets.

STRANDED COTTON

Thread used for embroidery.

TAPESTRY WOOL

Mainly used for tapestry and embroidery work.

QUILLING PAPER

Precision-cut strips of paper, available in 3 mm and 6 mm widths in a variety of colours. Available from art and craft shops.

Tracy Marsh uses and recommends quilling paper from Crafty Lady. Trade enquiries should be directed to: CRAFTY LADY
PO BOX 57
Clarendon, SA 5157.

QUILLING TOOL

A hat-pin or toothpick can be used in its place. Used to roll quilling paper.

PARAFILM

This self-sealing tape is used in floral arrangements, posies, and so on. The tape is stretched to adhere.

FLORIST WIRE

Gauge 22 to 26 wire is the most suitable. It is available from craft supply shops.

SILK FLOWERS

A wide variety of these flowers are available—for example, roses, buttercups, daisies, hydrangeas, heather, blossom, mixed posies, wisteria, violets, leaves, and so on.

FLORAL EMBROIDERY

Even if you have only the most basic needlework skills, with a little practice you will be able to sew these delicate flowers. By following the step-by-step instructions in this chapter, you can add a personal touch to all sorts of items, such as a hand-towel, painted windcheater, shirt collar, and fabric photograph frame (illustration 1).

Using commonly available materials and a little imagination, you can create original articles in just a few hours.

Illustration 1

The Basic Flower Stitches

Depending on the effect required, you can use either stranded cotton or tapestry wool for the flowers. For the finer flowers on the shirt collar and photograph frame, use stranded cotton divided into single strands, and a very small, fine needle. For the thicker flowers on the windcheater and hand-towel, use tapestry wool divided into two strands, and a larger, thicker needle.

The needle must not have a large eye—that is, it needs to be an even thickness right through to the eye (diagram 1).

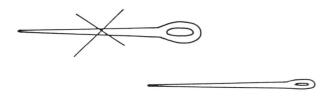

Diagram 1

Note: All the following instructions are for right-handed sewers. If you are left-handed, simply reverse the way of working.

GRUB ROSE

Using a darker coloured length of thread (stranded cotton or tapestry wool), pick up about 5 mm of fabric and wind the thread six or seven times around the needle (diagram 2). Place your thumb on the twisted thread, and pull the needle through the twist, holding it securely. Take the needle back to the point of entry (arrows in diagram 2) and insert next to the twist (or grub) for the second petal.

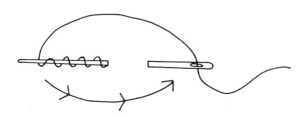

Diagram 2

Repeat for the second grub, laying it next to the first one (diagram 3). This forms the centre of the rose.

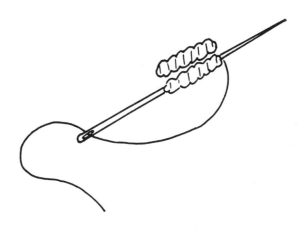

Diagram 3

Using a lighter coloured thread, insert the needle next to the two darker grubs, and bring it through on the opposite side. Wind the thread ten or eleven times around the needle, place your thumb on the twisted thread, and pull the needle through the twist, again holding it securely. Wrap the formed grub around the two darker grubs (diagram 4) by inserting the needle at point A, and bringing it up at point B.

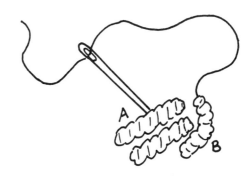

Diagram 4

Repeat these same steps, making more grubs, until the rose is the size you want.

Note: The grubs should overlap slightly to resemble the shape of a rose (illustration 1).

Illustration 1

LAZY DAISY

The lazy daisy is a combination of chain-stitch and a French knot. Bring the needle through the fabric for the centre of the daisy. Reinsert the needle in the same place and make a small stitch (about 5 mm), looping the thread under the needle. Anchor this loop with a short stitch (diagram 5), and bring the needle back to the centre of the flower. Repeat this four times, bringing the needle back to the centre each time, to form a five-petal daisy. Add a French knot for the centre.

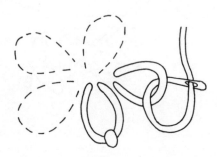

Diagram 5

SATIN-STITCH FLOWER

Bring the needle through the fabric for the centre of the flower. Reinsert the needle in the same place and make a small stitch (5 mm to 6 mm). Bring the needle back to the centre of the flower (diagram 6) and insert. Repeat the stitch twice in exactly the same place, to form one petal. Stitch another four petals in the same way, to complete the flower. Add a French knot for the centre.

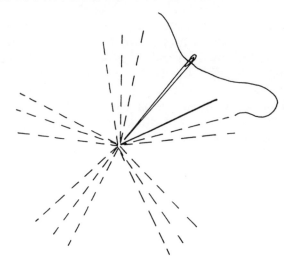

Diagram 6

FRENCH KNOT FLOWER

To make a French knot, pick up about 2 mm of fabric and wind the thread twice around the needle (diagram 7). Place your thumb on the twisted thread, and pull the needle through the twist, holding it securely. Take the needle back to the point of entry (arrows in diagram 7), and insert. Neatly sew six French knots in the shape of a flower (diagram 7).

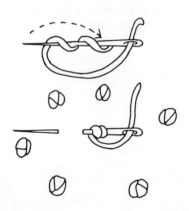

Diagram 7

Note: The French knot is also used for the centres of the lazy daisy and satin-stitch flower.

Add a touch of Spring to the Bathroom with an Embroidered Hand-Towel.

'Flowers For Sale' Stencil-Painting, combined with the Floral Embroidery, creates a delicate effect on this otherwise plain pink windcheater.

Keep the memory of that special moment displayed in the Embroidered Photograph Frame.

Create the Elegance of the Victorian Era with the finely Embroidered Shirt Collar.

Enjoy the fragrance of pot-pourri with the Perfumed Japanese Fan and Fragrant Hand-Mirror.

LEAF

The leaf is simply a single chain-stitch, as described in the lazy daisy instructions above.

STEM

The stems consist of a single stitch caught with a small stitch in the middle to curve them slightly.

Bring the needle through from the back of the fabric to the place where you would like the stem to start (point A). Insert the needle at the place where you would like the stem to end (point B), and bring it back up in the middle of the stem on the inside of the thread (diagram 8). Make a small stitch to anchor the thread. The curve of the stem depends on how far out the small stitch is put.

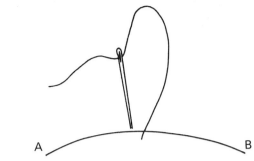

Diagram 8

Embroidered Hand-Towel

Materials Needed
>   6 skeins of tapestry wool, including green
>   plain coloured hand-towel
>   large needle
>   scissors
>   80 cm of 4 cm wide straight lace

To Make

Choose a suitable shade of wool for each flower, depending on the colour of the hand-towel. Remember that for the grub rose you need a lighter and a darker shade of wool, whereas for each of the other types of flower you use only one colour. Use easily manageable lengths of wool, divided into two strands. Use diagram 1 as a pattern guide for placement of the flowers.

It is not necessary to work the stitches in any particular order, but the leaves and stems should be done last. When you have finished the embroidery, trim each end of the hand-towel with the straight lace.

Illustration 1

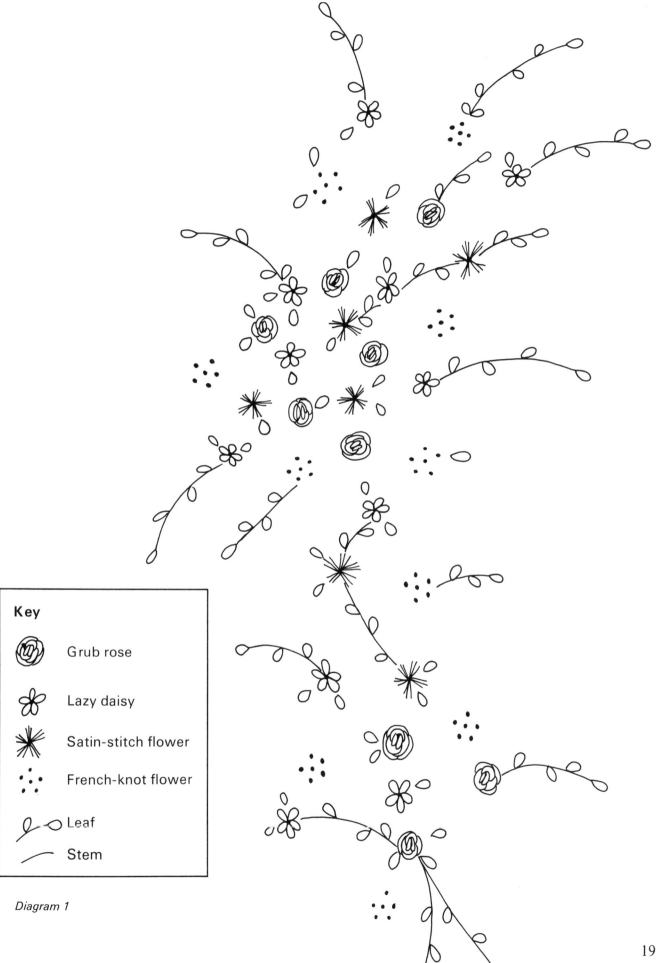

Key

🌀 Grub rose

✿ Lazy daisy

✳ Satin-stitch flower

⦂⦂ French-knot flower

🍃 Leaf

— Stem

Diagram 1

19

'Flowers for Sale' Embroidered Windcheater

Materials Needed
windcheater (painted)
6 skeins of tapestry wool, including green
large needle
scissors

To Make
See 'Flowers for Sale', on page 50, for step-by-step instructions on how to paint the windcheater. When you have finished the painting, choose six tapestry wools that will complement the colour-scheme used.

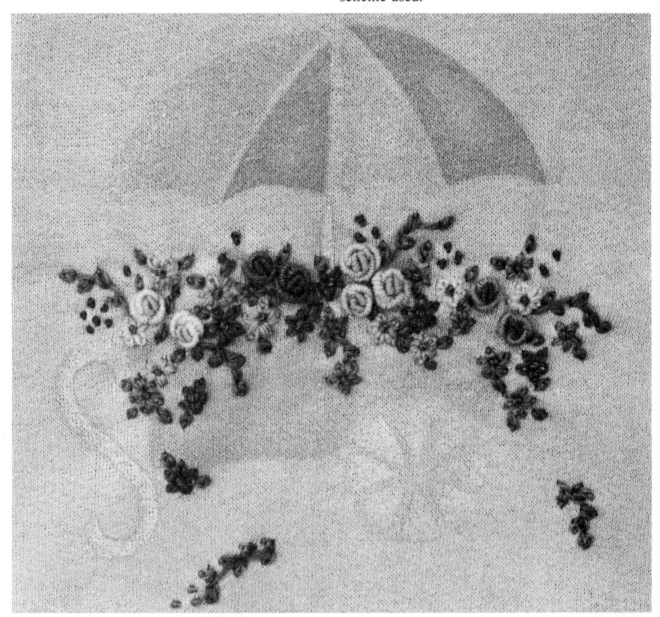

Illustration 1

20

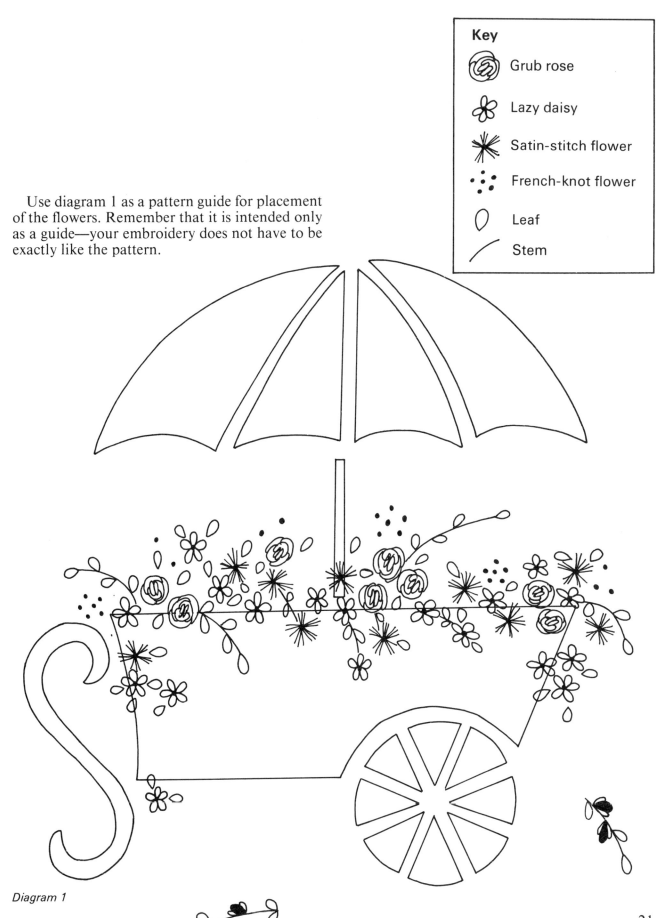

Key

Grub rose

Lazy daisy

Satin-stitch flower

French-knot flower

Leaf

Stem

Use diagram 1 as a pattern guide for placement of the flowers. Remember that it is intended only as a guide—your embroidery does not have to be exactly like the pattern.

Diagram 1

Embroidered Photograph Frame

Materials Needed

  scissors
  30 cm plain fabric
  pencil
  stranded cotton in 4 colours, including green
  small fine needle
  thick white pasteboard
  Stanley knife
  polyester wadding
  craft glue and brush
  contact adhesive
  10 cm narrow ribbon
  spray glue
  1.4 metres gathered lace

To Make

Cut a 25 cm × 30 cm piece of the fabric. Using the pencil, lightly transfer pattern A of the Lace Pot-Pourri Photograph Frame (page 00) on to the

Use diagram 1 as a pattern guide for placement of the flowers, and remember always to embroider on the side of the fabric without the pencil markings.

Make the grub roses first, using a darker shade of single-stranded cotton for the centre of each rose and a lighter shade for the outside. Sew the lazy daisies in a different colour. Finally, embroider all the leaves and stems in the green stranded cotton.

Illustration 1

Make up the photograph frame according to the instructions on page 32. The only difference is that instead of covering piece A with the lace and pot-pourri, you use the floral embroidery.

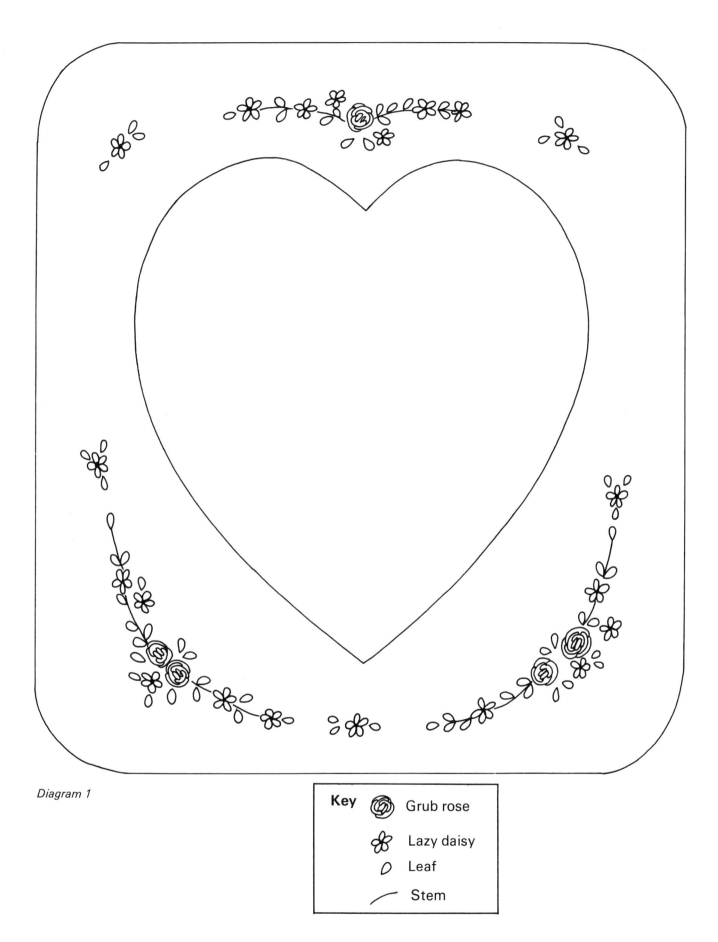

Diagram 1

Key		
	Grub rose	
	Lazy daisy	
	Leaf	
	Stem	

23

Embroidered Shirt Collar

Any clothing can be embroidered in the same way as this shirt—a simple and inexpensive method of revamping your wardrobe.

Materials Needed
    shirt with collar
    stranded cotton in 5 colours, including green
    very fine needle
    scissors
    gathered lace

To Make

Start your embroidery in the centre of the bottom edge of the shirt collar, using single strands of cotton. Use diagram 1 as a pattern guide for placement of the flowers.

Embroider the roses first, using a darker shade in the centre and a lighter shade on the outside. Next sew the lazy daisies in a different colour. Then sew the leaves in the green cotton. Last of all, embroider the French knots in a contrasting colour, including the centres of the lazy daisies.

Sew gathered lace around the edge of the collar to complete this very feminine look.

Note: You can also embroider shirt pockets to match the collars.

Illustration 1

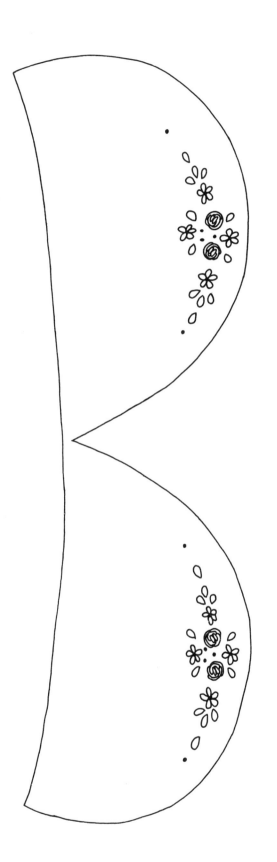

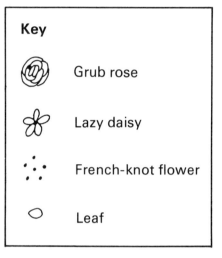

Key

Grub rose

Lazy daisy

French-knot flower

Leaf

Diagram 1

POT-POURRI
AND
LACE

Pot-Pourri

Pot-pourri—that delicious blend of heady fragrances—is made from many different scented flowers and herbs, dried and mixed with oils. The scents of the flowers last much longer when a fixative is added to the pot-pourri. The most common fixative is ground orris-root; dried lemon and orange rind can also be used.

The fragrances are further enhanced by adding oils such as rose, geranium, aphrodisia, jasmine, and boronia, and spices and herbs such as cinnamon, cloves, nutmeg, allspice, bay-leaves, and coriander. The following recipe for pot-pourri is both quick and easy to make.

Ingredients
    1 litre dried rose petals
    285 ml dried leaves
    285 ml dried lavender
    1 heaped teaspoon powdered orris-root
    6 bay-leaves
    14 g cloves
    1 teaspoon allspice
    55 g coarse salt

To Make

Mix the flowers, leaves, orris-root, and spices together. Arrange them in layers, in a jar, sprinkling salt between each layer. Cover the jar tightly and allow the mixture to mature for one month.

POT-POURRI MADE IN A MICROWAVE
With the help of a microwave oven, you can make this time-saving version of pot-pourri.

To Make

Pick the scented flowers and leaves on a dry day. Keeping each variety separate, break the large flowers into petals and remove the leaves from their stems. Spread each variety on a paper towel and sprinkle with a small amount of orris-root. Turn them over and coat the other side. You will need about 1 tablespoon of orris-root for each cup of petals. Cover the petals with another paper towel.

Dry each variety separately in the microwave oven on 'High'. The drying time will vary depending on the type and quantity of flowers—between 30 seconds and 3 minutes. Do not leave the flowers in the oven until they become crisp and crumbly.

Add a little extra orris-root, sprinkle with salt, and add crushed spices and herbs such as nutmeg, coriander seed, cinnamon stick, cloves, and vanilla bean. Mix well, and leave in an open container for one to two weeks, stirring daily.

Perfumed Japanese Fan

Materials Needed

pencil
thick white pasteboard
scissors
spray glue
polyester wadding
50 cm × 35 cm lace fabric
pot-pourri
contact adhesive
3 metres narrow ribbon
50 cm of 3 cm wide gathered lace
25 cm of 10 cm wide scalloped lace
50 cm × 35 cm fabric
small silk flowers

To Make

Trace the paper pattern, and transfer to the pasteboard, following the instructions given. Cut out the two pasteboard pieces. Lightly glue one piece to the wadding and leave to dry. Trim the wadding neatly around the edges of the pasteboard.

Cut out lace fabric to cover this piece, allowing an extra 3 cm around the edges. Spread a thin layer of pot-pourri to cover the top of the wadding evenly. Lay the fabric (right side up) over the pot-pourri (illustration 2), and carefully turn the fan piece over to the pasteboard side, making sure not to spill any of the pot-pourri.

Apply contact adhesive around the edges of the pasteboard and, as neatly as possible, bring all the lace fabric over and adhere to the pasteboard.

Decorate the front of the fan with strips of ribbon, using the full-size pattern as a guide.

Using contact adhesive, glue the gathered lace around the top of the pasteboard side of the fan (diagram 1).

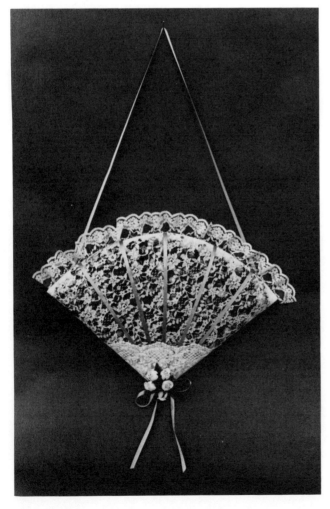

Illustration 1

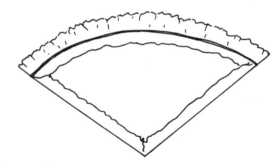

Diagram 1

Glue the scalloped lace across the base of the front of the fan, turning the ends over and gluing them to the back.

Cut fabric to cover the other pasteboard piece, 2 cm larger than the pattern. Using spray glue, stick the wrong side of the fabric to the pasteboard. Turn the fan piece over to the pasteboard side, apply contact adhesive around the edges, bring the fabric over, and adhere.

Using a compass or scissors, make two small holes on the fabric side of one of the pieces, in the

Illustration 2

position shown on the pattern. Cut off 90 cm of the ribbon, thread it through the holes, and knot at the back. Apply contact adhesive to the back of each piece and stick them together.

Glue the small silk flowers on to the base of the front of the fan, as shown in illustration 1. Tie the remaining ribbon into a bow and glue it under the silk flowers.

Lace Pot-Pourri Photograph Frame

Materials Needed
- pencil
- thick white pasteboard
- Stanley knife
- spray glue
- polyester wadding
- scissors
- 25 cm × 30 cm lace fabric
- 30 cm plain fabric
- craft glue and brush
- pot-pourri
- contact adhesive
- 1.4 metres gathered lace
- 10 cm narrow ribbon

To Make

Trace the paper patterns, and transfer to pasteboard, following the instructions given. Cut the five pieces needed, and carefully cut out the heart centre of piece A with a Stanley knife.

Lightly spray-adhere piece A on to the polyester wadding and leave to dry. Trim the wadding neatly around the edges of the pasteboard and carefully cut out the heart-shaped centre.

Cut out the lace fabric for piece A, making it 3 cm larger all round than the pattern. Cut pieces B and C from the plain fabric, allowing an extra 2 cm around the edges. Cut out the fabric for the stand (pieces D), 3 cm larger all round than the pattern.

BACKING PIECES

Paint craft glue (or spray glue) on one side of the pasteboard pieces B and C, and adhere to the centre of the wrong side of the fabric pieces, making sure to rub all creases out of the fabric. Turn over, and apply craft glue around the edges of the pasteboard. Bring the fabric over and adhere.

Illustration 1

FRONT

Spread a thin layer of pot-pourri to cover the wadding side of piece A evenly (illustration 2). Lay the lace fabric (right side up) over the pot-pourri, and carefully turn the frame piece over to the pasteboard side, making sure not to spill any of the pot-pourri.

Spread contact adhesive around the edges of the pasteboard and, as neatly as possible, bring the lace fabric over and adhere.

Pierce the heart centre of the lace with the sharp point of the scissors, and cut the fabric into 10 mm wide strips, being extremely careful to keep the cuts 2 mm away from the edge of the pasteboard (illustration 3).

Spread a thin layer of contact adhesive around the edges of the heart opening on the pasteboard side, pull the strips of fabric tightly over the edge,

The Lace Pot-pourri Photograph Frame displayed here amongst the scent of pot-pourri.

Capture the sweet scent of the garden—Scented Hoop Decoration.

For a special gift idea, make a Pot-pourri Bon-Bon.

Fragrant Garland Decorations, an effect welcome for any home.

Illustration 2

and adhere, pressing down. Using contact adhesive, decorate the outside edge and the heart opening, on the pasteboard side, with the gathered lace.

STAND

Glue each pasteboard piece on to the centre of the wrong side of each piece of fabric. Glue and fold as shown in diagram 1.

Glue and fold over sides   cut   Glue up bottom flap

Diagram 1

Illustration 3

33

Pierce a hole in the centre of one piece, thread the narrow ribbon through the fabric-covered side into the hole, and knot it at the back. Glue the backs of the stand pieces together with contact adhesive, including the material flaps at the top.

Place the bottom edge of the stand in line with the centre base of piece B on the fabric side. Draw a line the width of the top edge of the stand. Carefully slice along the line with a Stanley knife, cutting to exactly the width of the pasteboard stand (diagram 2). With the ribbon side of the stand facing the backing piece, slide the fabric flap through the cut.

Turn the backing over to the pasteboard side and glue the loose flap down. Pierce another hole in the backing, halfway between the base and the top of the stand, thread the ribbon through, and knot.

Apply contact adhesive to the pasteboard sides of both backing pieces, B and C, and carefully glue them together. Glue the pasteboard side of piece A to piece C, using contact adhesive. As diagram 3 shows, you leave part of the frame unglued, so that you can slip a photograph into the frame.

Diagram 2

Diagram 3

Fragrant Hand-Mirror

Materials Needed
pencil
scissors
corrugated cardboard
pasteboard
Stanley knife
40 cm fabric
polyester wadding
spray glue
pot-pourri
contact adhesive
1.2 metres of 2 cm wide gathered lace
craft glue and brush
50 cm narrow gathered lace
1 metre narrow braid
15 cm diameter round mirror

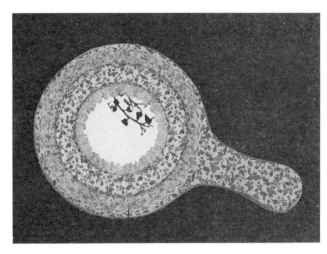

Illustration 1

To Make

Trace the paper patterns, and transfer them to the corrugated cardboard and pasteboard, following the instructions given. Use a Stanley knife to cut out the four pieces. Cut fabric for each of the cardboard base pieces, allowing an extra 3 cm around the edges, and also for the circular pieces, allowing an extra 2 cm.

Lightly glue the two circular pieces to the wadding with spray glue, and leave to dry. Trim the wadding neatly around the edges and carefully around the cut-out centre.

Spread a thin layer of pot-pourri to cover evenly the wadding side of the circle without the cut-out centre (illustration 2). Lay the fabric (right side up) over the pot-pourri, and carefully turn over to the pasteboard side, making sure not to spill any of the pot-pourri. Apply contact adhesive around the edges of the pasteboard and, as neatly as possible, bring all the fabric over and adhere to the pasteboard. Using contact adhesive, decorate around the edge of the wrong side with the wide gathered lace.

Spray-adhere the cut fabric to the wadding side of the circle with the cut-out centre. Turn over, brush craft glue around the edges of the pasteboard side, bring the fabric over, and adhere. Pierce the cut-out centre of the fabric with the sharp point of the scissors, and cut the fabric into

1 cm wide strips, being extremely careful to keep the cuts 2 mm away from the edge of the pasteboard. Spread a thin layer of craft glue around the edges of the opening on the pasteboard side, pull the strips of fabric tightly over the edge, and adhere.

Decorate the inside edge with the narrow gathered lace, and the outside edge with the wide gathered lace.

Illustration 2

BASE

Spray-adhere the fabric to each of the cardboard base pieces. Cut strips at 2 cm intervals around the fabric edges of the base pieces. Apply craft glue to the edges of the cardboard side, fold over the strips, and adhere (illustration 3).

Using contact adhesive, glue the base pieces together on the wrong sides. Glue the narrow braid around the edge to cover the join.

Position the mirror and adhere with the contact adhesive (illustration 4).

Centre and glue the piece with the cut-out centre around the mirror. Glue the pot-pourri piece on the other side of the mirror.

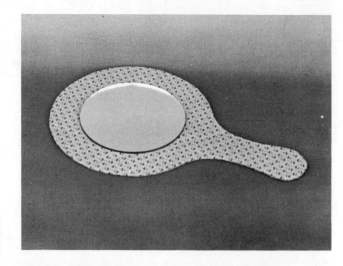

Illustration 3

Illustration 4

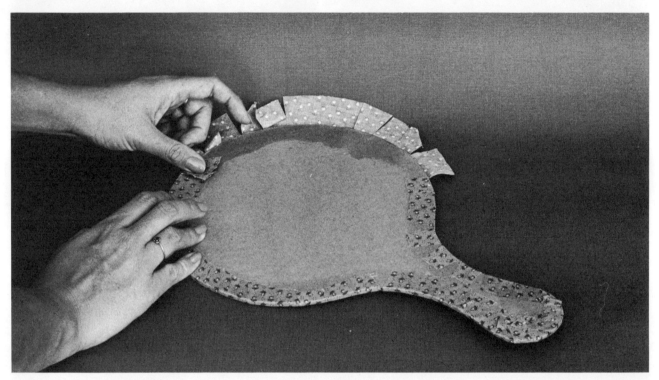

Scented Hoop Decoration

Fill your room with the sweet-smelling scent of pot-pourri, unusually displayed in an embroidery hoop. A hoop of any size can be used to make the Scented Hoop Decoration.

Materials Needed
embroidery hoop
lace fabric
scissors
pot-pourri
contact adhesive
gathered lace
silk flowers
narrow ribbon

To Make

Lay the embroidery hoop on the lace fabric and, allowing an extra 3 cm around the edges, cut out two circles.

Separate the hoop into its two parts by undoing the metal screw at the top. Place the inner wooden ring on a flat surface, and lay one piece of lace on top of it. Spread a layer of pot-pourri evenly over the lace. Place the other piece of lace on top of the pot-pourri. Very carefully slip the outer wooden ring back into position, and tighten the screw (illustration 2).

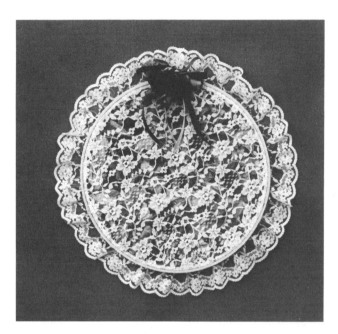

Illustration 1

Pull both pieces of lace tightly around the edges of the hoop to secure the pot-pourri in place. Turn over and carefully trim the excess fabric, leaving enough to glue the gathered lace on to the edges of the hoop with the contact adhesive. Glue the silk flowers to the top of the hoop and tie a ribbon bow on to the metal screw.

Illustration 2

Pot-Pourri Bon-Bon

Materials Needed
  scissors
  fabric
  cardboard cylinder from a toilet roll
  contact adhesive
  30 cm straight lace
  50 cm narrow ribbon
  pot-pourri
  15 cm lace or braid

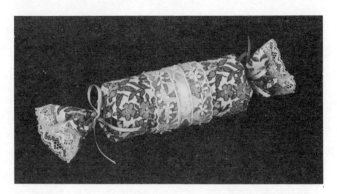

Illustration 1

To Make
Use the scissors to cut a piece of fabric 12 cm longer than the cardboard cylinder and 2 cm wider than its circumference. Glue 1 cm of the fabric at each end, and fold over to make a finished-off edge. Glue straight lace to the inside edge of each folded end (illustration 2).

Centre the cylinder lengthwise on the wrong side of the fabric and wrap the fabric around to enclose it, overlapping the edges. Glue along the full length of the cylinder to the lace ends. Leave to dry.

Gather the fabric at one end of the cylinder and tie 25 cm of the narrow ribbon tightly around it. Fill with the pot-pourri, gather the fabric at the open end, and tie the rest of the ribbon tightly around to secure it.

Decorate the centre of the bon-bon with the lace or braid.

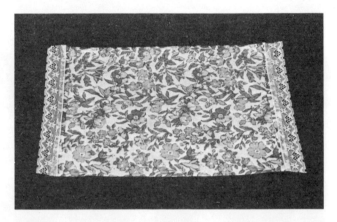

Illustration 2

Fragrant Garland Decoration

If you like the rustic look of a wreath or garland, but at the same time you long for the femininity of lace and the scent of pot-pourri, you can combine all three features in this Fragrant Garland Decoration (illustration 1).

Materials Needed

straw or grapevine wreath	florist wire
scissors	wire-cutters
35 mm wide ribbon	parafilm
15 mm wide ribbon or lace	10 mm wide florist ribbon
contact adhesive	narrow straight lace
organza	6 lavender stems
pot-pourri	1 bunch silk hydrangeas

Illustration 1

To Make

Measure the circumference of the wreath, and double it. Cut a piece of the 35 mm wide ribbon and a piece of the 15 mm wide ribbon or lace to this calculated measurement.

Glue one end of the 35 mm ribbon to the inside edge of the wreath, and evenly bind the ribbon around at 3 cm or 4 cm intervals. Trim the ribbon and bond to the starting-point (illustration 2).

Repeat this binding process with the 15 mm wide ribbon or lace, gluing it in the centre of the 35 mm ribbon. Cut two 25 cm lengths from the 35 mm ribbon and glue them to the base or top of the wreath (diagram 1).

Cut four 15 cm squares of organza. Place about 2 teaspoons of pot-pourri on each piece, and gather the organza up into a ball. Twist wire around each to form a stem, and trim off the excess organza. Tape the wire with parafilm, arrange the four balls in a diamond shape, and twist the wires together to hold them.

Make two ribbon loops and two lace loops. For each loop, loop the florist ribbon or lace backwards and forwards two or three times from the top to the bottom to the length required. Place a piece of wire over the centre of the loops, fold the ribbon loops over the wire, and twist firmly to

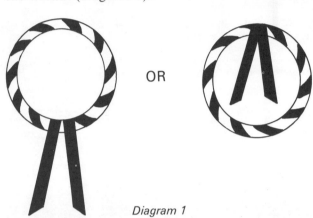

OR

Diagram 1

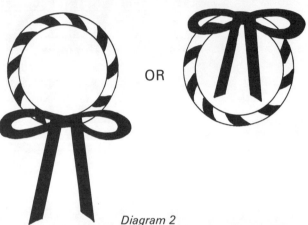

OR

Diagram 2

Repeat with the 15 mm ribbon or lace, gluing it over the ribbon. Cut two more 25 cm lengths from the 35 mm ribbon and glue these to form loops on the wreath (diagram 2).

Repeat with the 15 mm ribbon or lace, but glue these so that they are at a slightly higher angle than the ribbon loops.

hold them tightly. Position them around the pot-pourri balls.

Arrange the six lavender stems and the silk hydrangeas around the balls. Secure with parafilm. Trim the stem of the posy to only 2 cm and wire it to the centre of the wreath over the ribbons (illustration 1).

Illustration 2

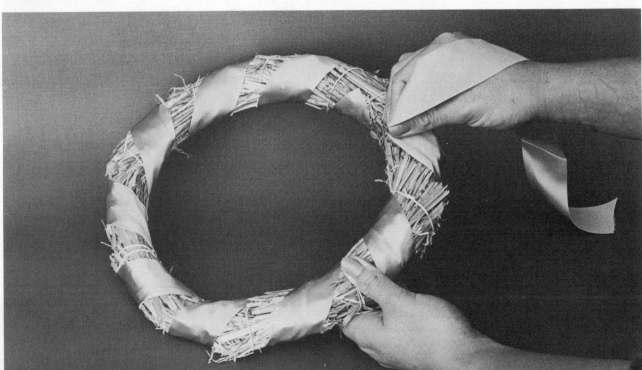

PAINTER'S PALETTE

Fabric-painting by the stencilling technique is a very versatile craft. The method is fun, easy, and, above all, it enables you to achieve a professional-looking painting with a minimum amount of time and effort. Once having cut the basic stencil, you can use it on a wide range of fabrics, as the examples in illustration 1 show.

Plastic stencils are easy to clean, and can be used over and over again with other paint colours. Stencil-painting can also be combined with embroidery to create a very delicate effect on an otherwise plain T-shirt or windcheater.

The following pages give instructions for four different fabric-painting designs. Alternatively, you can use the method to create your own designs.

Illustration 1

Floral Bouquets

Materials Needed

    pencil
    thin plastic sheeting
    cardboard
    small craft knife
    T-shirt or windcheater
    masking tape
    fabric paints in 3 colours, including green
    china plate
    medium stencil brush
    fine paintbrush
    iron
    2.5 metres narrow ribbon
    sewing thread (same colour as ribbon)
    needle
    scissors

To Make

Using a pencil, trace the Floral Bouquets stencil pattern on to plastic sheeting. It is not necessary for the pencil lines to be marked on the plastic, provided that the indentations are clear.

Put the plastic on the cardboard and, holding the craft knife as you would a pencil, cut along the traced lines, turning the plastic sheeting rather than the knife. For smooth edges, cut each shape without lifting the knife. Move slowly, always cutting towards yourself. If you make a mistake in

Illustration 1

cutting, mend it with transparent tape, and recut. Place the cardboard under the T-shirt or windcheater, and mask off the seven small leaves on the stencil with masking tape (illustration 2).

Illustration 2

Illustration 3

Position the stencil on the fabric, and tape it in place. Pour a small amount of the paint into the china plate. Dip the stencil brush into the paint, and then dab the bristles on to a scrap of cardboard to remove excess paint. Continue until the brush is almost dry. Using a quick up-and-down motion, paint around the edges of the flower petals first. To add depth to your painting, build up the paint in layers.

When you have painted all the flowers, remove the stencil and transfer it to another position (illustration 3).

When you have painted about five bouquets on the garment, remove the masking from the leaves, and mask the flowers with new tape. Paint the leaves with the green paint.

Use the fine paintbrush to complete the design. Using green paint, draw in stems to connect all the flowers and leaves, then paint the small dotted flowers in a contrasting colour (diagram 1).

When the designs have dried thoroughly, iron the reverse side of the fabric for 2 or 3 minutes to heat-set them. The paintings will then be fast and washable.

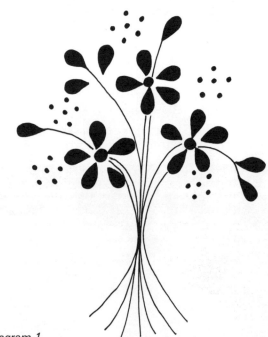

Diagram 1

Tie a small bow from the narrow ribbon for each bouquet and neatly hand-stitch over the stems of the bouquet.

Roses

Materials Needed
- pencil
- thin plastic sheeting
- cardboard
- small craft knife
- T-shirt or windcheater
- sponge
- masking tape
- fabric paints in green, white, light and dark shades for the roses, and a contrasting colour
- china plate
- medium stencil brush
- fine paintbrush
- scissors
- assorted leaves and ferns—e.g. rose leaves, asparagus fern, daisy leaves, maidenhair, vine-leaves, peacock fern
- iron

Illustration 1

To Make

Using a pencil, trace the Roses stencil pattern on to the plastic sheeting. It is not necessary for the pencil lines to be marked on the plastic, provided that the indentations are clear.

Put the plastic on the cardboard and, holding the craft knife as you would a pencil, cut along the traced lines, turning the sheet rather than the knife. For smooth edges, cut each shape without lifting the knife. Move slowly, always cutting towards yourself. If you make a mistake in cutting, mend it with transparent tape, and recut.

Place the cardboard under the T-shirt or windcheater, and slightly dampen the fabric with a clean sponge. Mask off the five rose-buds on the stencil with masking tape, position the stencil on the fabric, and tape it in place. Mix a small amount of the light-coloured paint for the roses on the china plate. Dip the stencil brush into the paint, and then dab the bristles on to a scrap of cardboard to remove excess paint. Using a quick up-and-down motion, paint in the roses on the stencil.

Unmask the rose-buds and paint them in the same way, using the dark rose colour. Remove the stencil.

Using the fine paintbrush, carefully fill in the petals with the dark rose colour (illustration 2).

Illustration 2

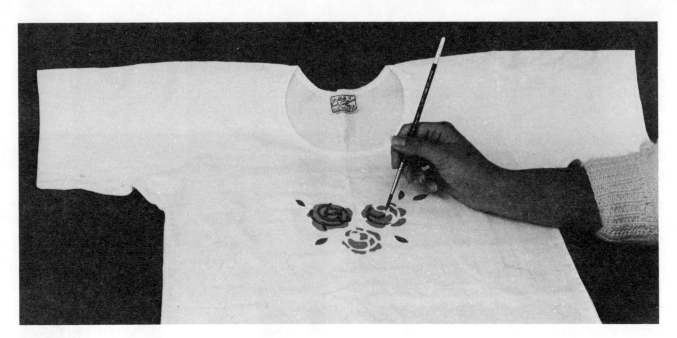

Illustration 3

Illustration 4

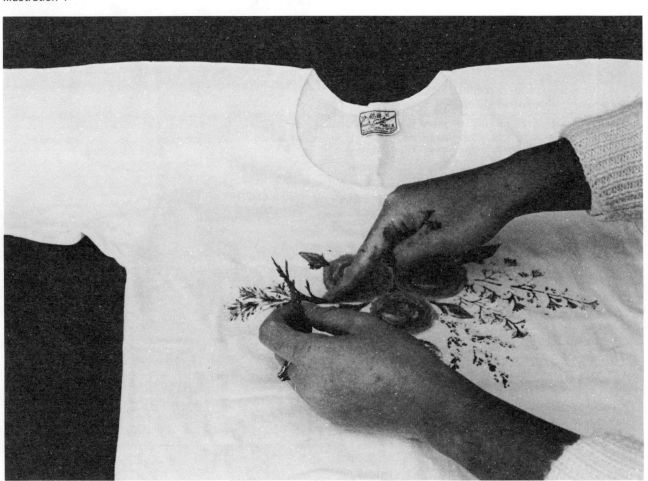

Next, use the light rose colour to enlarge the roses and buds so that they resemble cabbage roses in full bloom. Complete the roses by highlighting the centres with white paint (illustration 3).

Carefully paint in the sepals of the buds with the green paint.

For the greenery around the roses, use an assortment of leaves and ferns. Paint each one with a thin layer of green fabric paint, and press them, one at a time, on to the fabric (illustration 4).

Use the contrasting colour to paint small daisies branching out from the roses (diagram 1 and illustration 1).

When the design has dried thoroughly, iron the reverse side of the fabric for 2 or 3 minutes to heat-set it. The painting will then be fast and washable.

Diagram 1

Teddy Bears' Picnic

Materials Needed
- pencil
- thin plastic sheeting
- cardboard
- small craft knife
- T-shirt or windcheater
- fabric paints in 5 colours, including black and brown
- china plate
- medium stencil brush
- masking tape
- fine paintbrush
- iron
- stranded embroidery cotton (same colours as balloon paints)
- needle
- scissors
- 2 metres narrow ribbon
- sewing thread (same colour as ribbon)

Illustration 1

To Make

Using a pencil, trace the Teddy Bears' Picnic stencil pattern on to the plastic sheeting. It is not necessary for the pencil lines to be marked on the plastic, provided that the indentations are clear.

Put the plastic on the cardboard and, holding the craft knife as you would a pencil, cut along the traced lines, turning the sheet rather than the knife. For smooth edges, cut each shape without lifting the knife. Move slowly, always cutting towards yourself. If you make a mistake in cutting, mend it with transparent tape, and recut.

Place the cardboard under the T-shirt or windcheater, position the stencil on the fabric, and tape it in place. Pour a small amount of the brown paint on to the china plate. Dip the stencil brush into the paint, and then dab the bristles on to a scrap of cardboard to remove excess paint. Continue until the brush is almost dry.

Using a quick up-and-down motion, and holding the brush so that it is perpendicular to the fabric, paint around the edges of the bear first. To achieve a shaded effect, build up the paint in layers—making it darker around the edges (illustration 2).

Transfer the stencil to a different position on the fabric, and repeat the process used for the first bear.

Illustration 2

Return the stencil to the original position, and mask off two of the three balloons on the stencil with masking tape. Choose a suitable colour, and paint the balloon in the same way as for the bears, shading it darker around the edges. Repeat for the other two balloons, painting each one a different colour. Repeat for the other bears.

Use the fine paintbrush and black fabric paint to paint in the bears' faces (diagram 1).

Diagram 1

When the designs have dried thoroughly, iron the reverse side of the fabric for 2 or 3 minutes to heat-set them. The paintings will then be fast and washable.

Thread 10 cm of matching embroidery cotton to the base of each balloon, and knot both ends to form the balloon strings (illustration 3).

Hand-stitch the balloon strings together on the bear's paw. Tie a small bow from the ribbon and stitch it neatly over the strings. Repeat for the other bears.

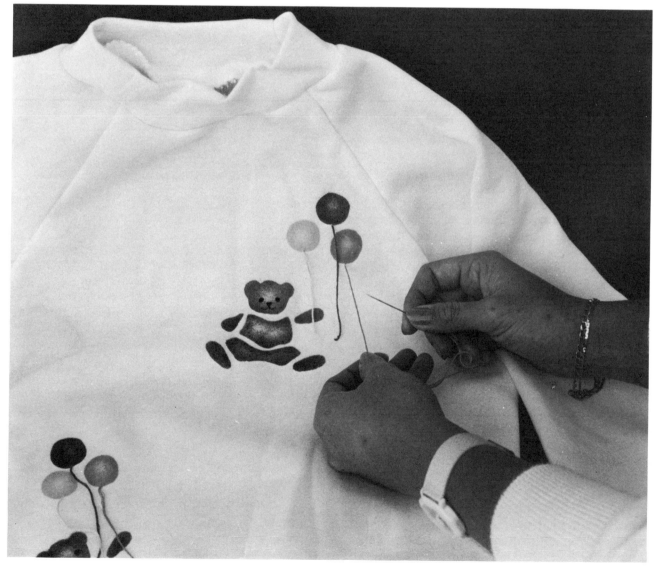

Illustration 3

'Flowers for Sale'

Materials Needed
> pencil
> thin plastic sheeting
> cardboard
> small craft knife
> T-shirt or windcheater
> masking tape
> fabric paints, in 3 colours
> china plate
> medium stencil brush
> iron
> scissors
> tapestry wools in assorted colours, including green
> large needle

To Make

Using a pencil, trace the 'Flowers for Sale' stencil pattern on to the plastic sheeting. It is not necessary for the pencil lines to be marked, provided that the indentations are clear.

Put the plastic on the cardboard and, holding the craft knife as you would a pencil, cut along the traced lines, turning the sheet rather than the knife. For smooth edges, cut each shape without lifting the knife. Move slowly, always cutting towards yourself. If you make a mistake in cutting, mend it with transparent tape, and recut.

Place the cardboard under the T-shirt or windcheater and mask off alternate sections of the umbrella, the pole, the wheel, and the handle with masking tape. For example, you may choose to paint the cart and two sections of the umbrella first (illustration 2).

Position the stencil on the fabric, and tape it in place. Pour a small amount of paint into the china plate. Dip the stencil brush into the paint, and then dab the bristles on to a scrap of cardboard to remove excess paint. Continue until the brush is almost dry.

Using small dabbing motions, paint around the edges of sections first. To achieve a shaded effect, build up the paint in layers—making it darker around the edges.

Illustration 1

Remove the masking tape, and tape over the painted sections. Paint the other parts of the umbrella in the same way, using a different colour.

Finally, paint the pole, wheel, and handle with the third colour.

When the design has dried thoroughly, iron the reverse side of the fabric for 2 or 3 minutes to heat-set it. The painting will then be fast and washable.

FLORAL EMBROIDERY

See the chapter 'Floral Embroidery', at the beginning of this book, for instructions on sewing flowers and foliage on to the 'Flowers for Sale' fabric-painting (illustration 3).

Illustration 2

Illustration 3

Paint this delightful 'Floral Bouquets' windcheater.

Any child would love to wear this 'Teddy Bears' Picnic suit.

The 'Roses' painted T Shirt—just perfect for a garden party.

Add a touch of lace and flowers to create romantic wedding accessories.

FRILLS
AND
FLOWERS

Lacy Parasol

This exquisite parasol can be used as a decorating feature, or carried as a charming old-world touch for a bride or bridesmaid.

Materials Needed
craft knife
28 cm rice-paper parasol
paper
pencil
scissors
50 cm lace fabric
contact adhesive
2 metres of 5 cm wide gathered lace
2 metres of 12 mm wide ribbon
silk flowers

To Make

Using the craft knife, carefully cut all the rice-paper from the parasol frame (illustration 2).

Lay the parasol frame on a piece of paper and draw around the outside of three adjoining sections to form one complete pattern. Count the number of sections in the whole frame and divide by three to work out how many pattern pieces will be needed to cover the parasol.

Using the pattern, cut panels from the lace fabric, allowing an extra 2 cm all round. Glue along the top edge of four adjoining bamboo struts, rubbing the glue in until it is tacky. Place the lace panel over the three sections of the parasol. Rub until the lace is adequately adhered. When dry, use scissors to trim the lace back to the bamboo on all sides (illustration 3).

Repeat the process until the entire parasol is covered in lace.

Glue the gathered lace around the inside edge of the parasol. Tie 1 metre of the ribbon around the handle, and the other metre around the top of the parasol. Decorate with silk flowers, attaching them to the parasol with contact adhesive.

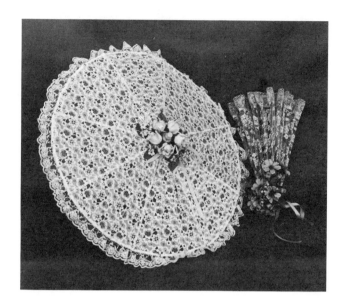

Illustration 1

Illustration 2

Illustration 3

56

Granny Lidded Basket

This novel basket, made by the soft sculpture technique, can be used for many purposes.

Materials Needed

  ruler
  25 cm diameter round basket
  compass
  pencil
  thick white pasteboard
  scissors
  polyester wadding or 10 mm foam-sheeting
  spray glue
  50 cm fabric
  craft glue and brush
  80 cm of 3 cm wide gathered lace
  contact adhesive
  nylon pantihose (suntan shade)
  polyester fibrefill
  sewing thread, in flesh colour and red
  needle
  2 small eyes
  make-up blusher
  50 cm narrow ribbon
  florist wire
  flesh-coloured felt
  pipe-cleaner (30 cm long)
  1 metre of 5 cm wide straight lace
  miniature basket of flowers

Illustration 1

To Make

BASKET LID

Place the ruler across the top of the basket and measure the diameter. Set the compass at half this measurement, and use to draw two circles on the pasteboard. Cut out the two circles and lay them on the top of the basket to check the size.

Stick one pasteboard circle to the foam or wadding with spray glue, and neatly trim the foam back to the edge of the pasteboard. Cut a piece of fabric, 3 cm larger all round than the pasteboard, and lightly adhere to the foam side with spray glue. Turn on to the pasteboard side and brush craft glue around the edges. Neatly pull the fabric over and stick down. Decorate around the edge of the wrong side with gathered lace.

Cut a piece of fabric 3 cm larger than the other pasteboard circle, and glue it to the pasteboard. Turn on to the pasteboard side, and brush craft glue around the edges. Tightly pull the fabric over and stick down. Glue to the pasteboard side of the padded circle with contact adhesive.

LINING THE BASKET

Place the compass in the centre of the basket and spread it out until it reaches the point at which the basket starts to curve at the sides. This will give the size for the base piece.

Place the compass on the pasteboard. Draw the circle and cut it out. Stick this piece to the foam or wadding with spray glue, and neatly trim the foam back to the edge of the pasteboard. Cut a piece of fabric 3 cm larger all round than the pasteboard circle, and lightly glue it to the foam side with spray glue. Turn on to the pasteboard side, and brush craft glue around the edges. Pull the fabric over, and adhere.

To line the inside of the basket, measure the circumference of the top and add 5 cm, to calculate the length of fabric needed. To work out the depth, place the finished base piece in the basket, measure from the top edge down to just below the base piece, and add 3 cm. If possible, cut the strip of fabric so that it has one long selvedge. For a finished edge, glue and fold the fabric on one of the short ends back about 10 mm.

Completely cover the top edge of the basket with craft glue or contact adhesive. Starting with the finished edge, glue the selvedge fabric to the top of the rim of the basket. Line the basket completely. Finally, place the raw edge under the finished edge and glue at the top and down the side.

Glue the centre of the base of the basket and gradually pleat and glue the fabric evenly around the basket. For neatness, pleat all the fabric in the same direction.

GRANNY

Cut a 12 cm square from the pantihose. Roll a tiny ball of polyester fibrefill for the nose, place it in the centre of the square, and stretch the pantihose tightly around it. Wrap the flesh-coloured thread several times around the nose, keeping it taut, and tie securely. Thread the needle with the flesh-coloured thread and sew running stitches around the square, 5 mm from the edge.

Stuff a handful of fibrefill into the gathered square, pull the thread tightly (keeping the nose centred), and sew several small stitches to secure. Use the needle to mould the fibrefill into a more detailed face (illustration 2).

To attach the eyes, sew from the back of the face to the front, directly above the cheek, and thread on one small eye (illustration 3). Sew back through the face, close to where the needle came out, pulling very tightly; take a few stitches to hold. Repeat for the other eye.

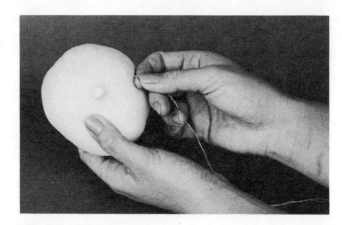

Illustration 2

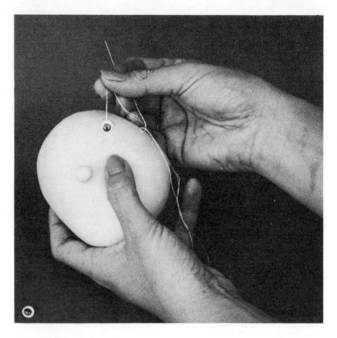

Illustration 3

To stitch the mouth: using the red sewing thread, bring the needle from the back of the head to the centre front of the face, halfway between the nose and the chin (point A in diagram 1).

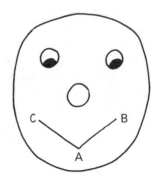

Diagram 1

58

Make one long, slightly upward stitch, over approximately quarter the width of the face (point B). Bring the needle out at the back of the face. Repeat twice. Repeat for the other side of the mouth, stitching from point A to point C. Carefully apply make-up blusher to the cheeks, nose, and chin.

Glue a small handful of fibrefill on to the back of the head for hair. Gather a small section of the hair into a bun, wrap the narrow ribbon around it, and secure (illustration 4).

Illustration 4

Mould the wire to make a small pair of glasses, and glue them over the eyes.

ARMS

Cut two rectangles of felt, 12 mm × 40 mm. Fold each piece in half, and glue on either end of the pipe-cleaner. Carefully trim around the ends of the felt to give a rounded appearance. Cut a piece of the fabric 30 cm × 5 cm. If possible, cut so that the strip of fabric has one long selvedge. Glue 1 cm of the fabric on either side, and fold over to give a finished-off edge.

Lay the felt-covered pipe-cleaner lengthwise on the wrong side of the fabric (illustration 5). Carefully glue and wrap the fabric around the pipe-cleaner to form the arms. Overlap the fabric with the selvedge on the outside.

Cut an 8 cm × 1 metre strip of the fabric; if possible, cut so that the strip has one long selvedge. Position the 5 cm wide straight lace in line with the raw edge of the strip of fabric. Stitch, 10 mm in from the edge, gathering the lace and fabric at the same time. Stitch or tie off securely.

Curve the covered pipe-cleaner around to form the arms, and glue them in the centre of the padded lid with contact adhesive.

Glue the prepared lace and fabric strip on top of the arms, and then glue the head on top of this with contact adhesive. Bend the arms into position, and slip the miniature basket of flowers over one arm.

Illustration 5

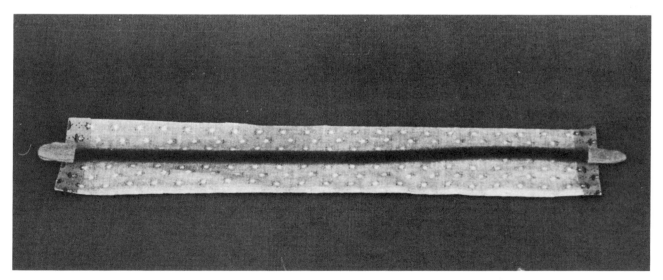

Fan Bouquet

This elegant Fan Bouquet is a way of adding a delightful personal touch to a wedding ceremony, either as a pretty accessory for the bride to carry, or as pew decorations.

Materials Needed

florist wire
12 silk rose-buds
wire-cutters
parafilm
12 silk ivy leaves
1 stem of silk mini buttercups or similar silk flowers
1.5 metres narrow ribbon
1.5 metres narrow ribbon, in a contrasting colour
2.8 metres narrow straight lace
scissors
dried gypsophila
1.3 metres of 7 mm wide ribbon
1.3 metres of 7 mm wide ribbon, in a contrasting colour
contact adhesive
lace fan

Illustration 1

To Make

Twist wire around the base of each silk rose-bud, leaving a 15 cm stem of wire. Wrap the wire with parafilm. Repeat for the silk ivy leaves and the mini buttercups.

Position the rose-buds in a fan-like shape, twisting the stems together to keep them in place (diagram 1).

Place the ivy leaves and the buttercups, one at a time, around the rose-buds, positioning them evenly, but still keeping the fan-shaped effect. Wrap the stems with parafilm to hold them in place.

Make loops, one from each of the two different-coloured narrow ribbons, and one from 1.5 metres of the straight lace. Loop the ribbon or lace backwards and forwards two or three times from the top to the bottom to the length required (illustration 2). Cut off the remainder of the ribbon.

Place a piece of wire over the centre of the

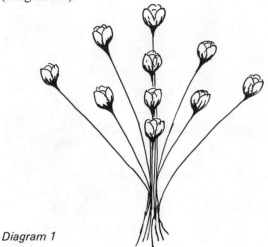

Diagram 1

Illustration 2

loops, fold the ribbon loops over the wire, and twist firmly to hold them tight. Make four wired loops in each of the ribbons and the lace, and position them evenly around the flowers. Wrap the stems with parafilm to hold them in place. Add dried gypsophila to fill in the arrangement, and again wrap the stems with parafilm.

Make three large wired bows, one from each of the 7 mm wide ribbons, and one from the remaining lace. Make a figure of eight for each bow, leaving adequate lengths on the ends. Place the wire across the centre, fold the ribbon or lace over the wire, and twist tightly. Bind the wires with parafilm. Attach the bows to the base of the arrangement with parafilm. Trim the stem to only 2 cm long. Apply contact adhesive to the back of the arrangement, and carefully glue it on to the lace fan.

Hot-Air Balloon

Materials Needed

15 cm polystyrene foam ball
pencil
Stanley knife
30 cm × 30 cm plain fabric
30 cm × 30 cm floral fabric
small screwdriver or nail-file
scissors
contact adhesive
5 metres of lace or braid
1.5 metres of 2 cm wide ribbon
3 metres narrow ribbon
10 cm diameter small basket
1 pin

To Make

Mark the foam ball into eight equal sections with fine pencil lines. Using the Stanley knife, cut into each of the pencilled lines the full length of the blade.

Cut the fabric into eight pieces, 2 cm larger all round than the actual foam sections—four pieces in the plain fabric and four pieces in the floral fabric. With the small screwdriver or nail-file, carefully push one piece of fabric into the cut foam, to cover one section of the ball completely. Trim excess fabric with scissors, and push the rest into the ball. Repeat this process, alternating plain and floral fabrics, until the ball is fully covered.

Using the contact adhesive, glue the lace or braid between each of the sections, and glue the 2 cm wide ribbon around the middle of the ball.

Cut the narrow ribbon into four 30 cm strips, and glue the end of one on to every second section around the middle of the ball (on top of the wide ribbon). Tie the remaining 2 cm ribbon into four bows, and glue one over each strip, to hide the ends.

Glue the free end of each ribbon strip on to the outside rim of the basket, making sure to glue them on straight (illustration 2).

Illustration 1

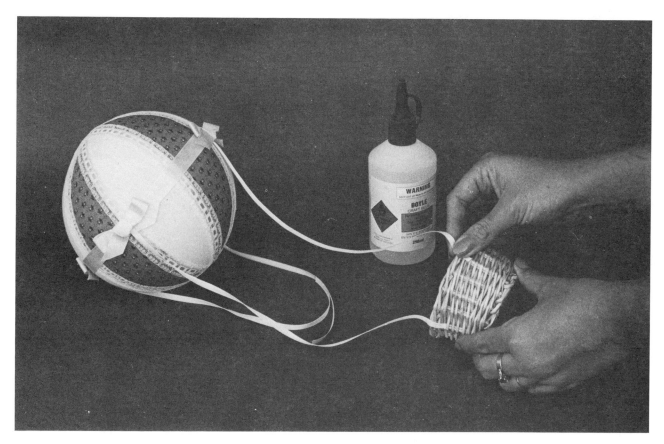

Illustration 2

Cut the rest of the lace or braid into twenty-two equal lengths. Glue six of these to form a star shape on the top of the ball, looping each one over and gluing it separately (illustration 3).

Cut an 80 cm length of narrow ribbon, and thread a pin through the ends to form a loop with which to hang the balloon. Push the pin through the middle of the star on top of the ball, to secure the loop.

Loop and glue each of the remaining sixteen pieces of lace or braid into four cross shapes over the ribbons on the basket. Tie bows with the narrow ribbon, and glue one over the centre of each cross shape around the basket (illustration 1).

Note: You can also make miniature hot-air balloons for mobiles and so on.

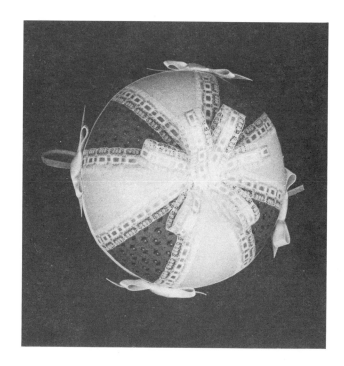

Illustration 3

PRESSED-FLOWER CRAFTS

Everyone loves fresh flowers, but our enjoyment is often marred by the fact that they must finally die. We can therefore appreciate the clever technique of preserving and displaying pressed flowers that will allow us to treasure the beauty of flowers for a lifetime.

Almost any blooms can easily be turned into decorative and useful items such as the Covered Diary, Floral Design Lightshade, Pressed-Flower Tissue-Box Cover, Pressed-Flower Picture Frame, and Scented Floral Candles (illustration 1).

The following pages give step-by-step instructions on pressing flowers and fashioning them into attractive crafts. No special equipment is needed: all you have to do is to keep the flowers and leaves under a weight for a few weeks. You can use a thick book, but a flower-press is the neatest and most efficient way of pressing flowers.

Illustration 1

Choosing and Pressing Flowers

CHOOSING FLOWERS

Most flowers are suitable for pressing, except for very fleshy blooms with a lot of moisture, or those with thick centres. White blooms often become translucent after pressing, whereas pink, blue, yellow, orange, and purple flowers all dry to a very 'antique' hue. Some red flowers change to an unattractive brown. It is advisable to test all flowers before using them. The following flowers press well:

violets	phlox
geraniums	azaleas
pansies	daisies
roses	primulas
buttercups	zinnias
fuchsias	larkspurs
hydrangeas	verbena
poppies	cosmos

Always press the flowers as soon as possible after picking or they will wilt. Never press damp petals.

CHOOSING LEAVES

Choose only the small leaves of large-leaved plants. Avoid the fleshy leaves of African violets and succulents. Press stems of flowers as well to add to your own design. The following leaves will press well:

ferns	asparagus fern
baby's tears	rose leaves
grape ivy	grasses

Illustration 1

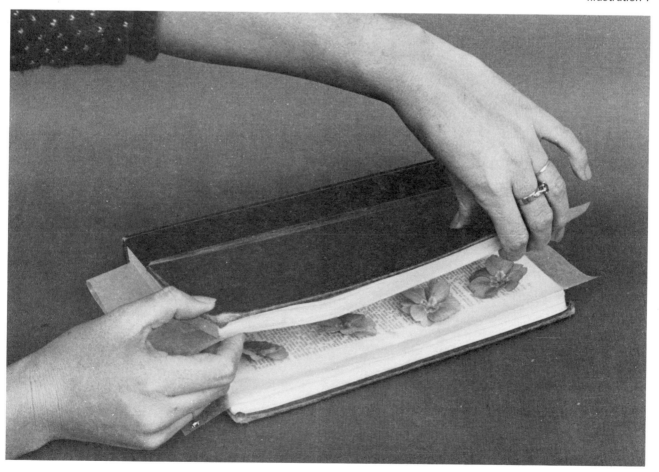

PRESSING FLOWERS AND LEAVES

Materials Needed
- assorted flowers and leaves
- blotting-paper
- tweezers
- flower-press or thick book

To Press

Carefully remove all the stems, and separate double blooms into single petals.

If using a flower-press, place blooms of the same type on the supplied sheets of blotting-paper, spacing the flowers with tweezers so that they are not touching. Cover the flowers with another sheet of blotting-paper. Layer these pairs of blotting-paper and flowers between the sheets of corrugated cardboard, and place them all in the press. Insert the four bolts and tighten the wings. Leave in a dry, airy place for two to four weeks.

If using a thick book, place single flowers and leaves between two sheets of blotting-paper. Group different varieties of flowers on separate sheets for even thickness. Place the blotters between the pages of the book next to the binding, and slowly roll the pages of the book over the blotting-paper (illustration 1).

Repeat for other layers of flowers, allowing at least 2 cm of pages between sheets of blotting-paper. Put the book in a warm, dry place and weight it down to ensure that neither light nor air can reach the flowers. Leave for two to four weeks.

The Hot-Air Balloon—so
simple and adorable.

Delight in the many uses of the Granny Lidded Basket.

Discover the everlasting beauty of Pressed Flowers. These craft ideas will compliment the decor of any home.

Send that special message in a Quilled Floral Bouquet card.

A selection of 'TOUCH OF BOUQUET' crafts.

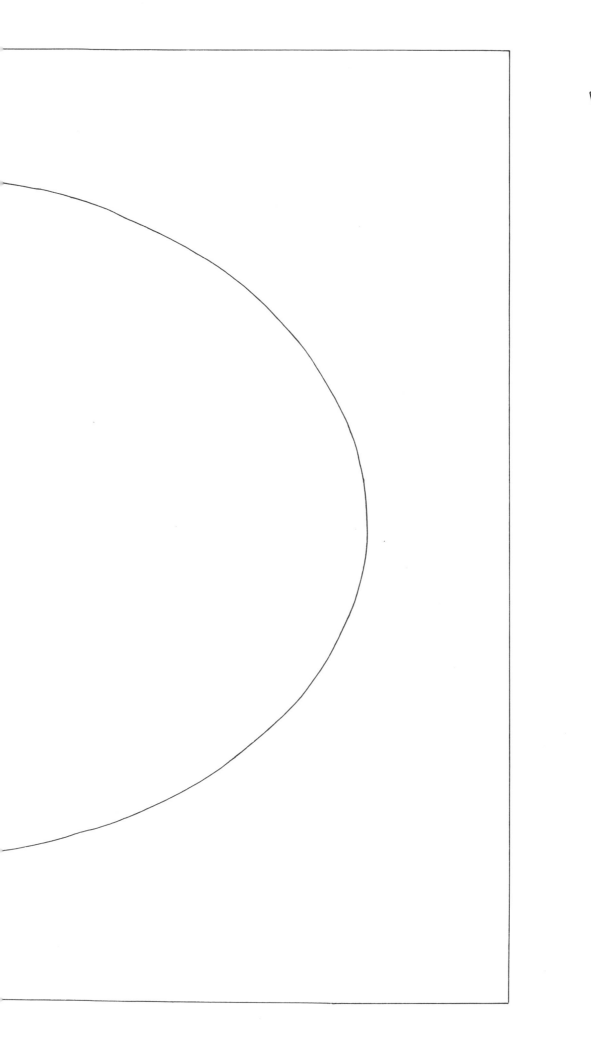

Roses
Stencil Pattern

Teddy Bears' Picnic
Stencil Pattern

Floral Bouquets
Stencil Pattern

Covered Diary

Materials Needed
- polyester wadding
- hard-cover diary
- scissors
- spray glue
- plain cotton fabric
- fusible webbing (cobweb)
- white organza
- pencil
- assorted pressed flowers, leaves, and stems
- tweezers
- iron
- craft glue and brush

Illustration 1

To Make

Cut a piece of wadding to fit the outside covers of the diary. Spray-adhere the wadding to the diary, and trim back any overlapping edges.

Open the diary to the middle pages and lay it on the fabric. Cut out the fabric, allowing an extra 3 cm around the edges. Cut the fusible webbing and the organza to the same size as the fabric. Wrap the cotton fabric around the outside of the diary, and lightly pencil in the positioning of the flowers.

Lay the fabric out flat, and arrange the pressed flowers over the pencil markings (illustration 2). Using the tweezers to move the flowers, adjust the arrangement until you are quite happy with it.

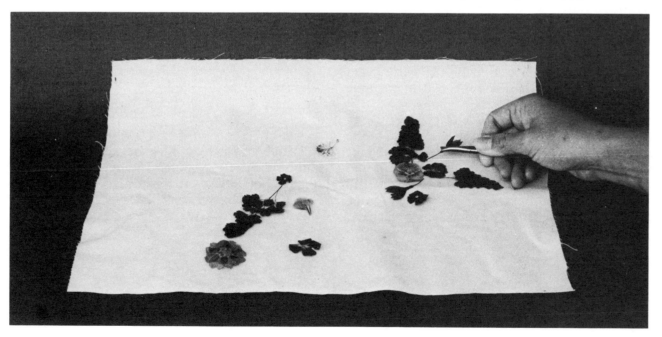

Illustration 2

69

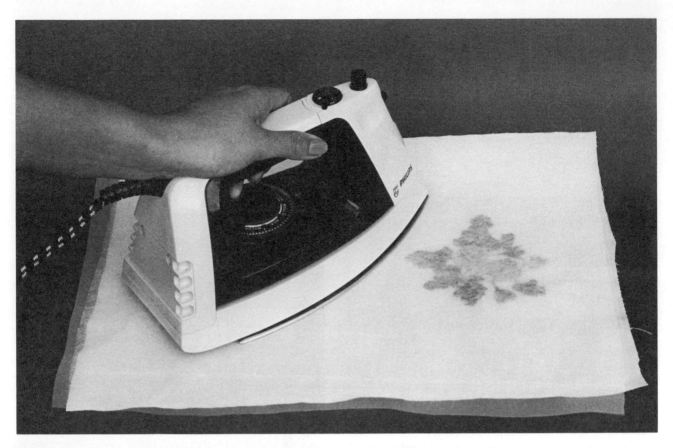

Illustration 3

Carefully lay first the fusible webbing, and then the organza, exactly on top of the cotton fabric. Set the iron heat-control to 'Wool' and heat-set the three fabrics, fusing the fabric and organza together (illustration 3).

Lay the fabric out flat, with the flower side facing down. Spray-glue the wadding on the back cover of the diary and attach it to the plain half of the fabric, positioning it with the extra 3 cm around the edges. Glue the front cover in the same way.

Open the diary to the inside front cover. Bring the two corners and the side fabric over on to the inside cover, and stick down with craft glue. Make two small cuts in the fabric, near the top and bottom of the centre binding. Glue the top and bottom fabric on to the inside cover (diagram 1). Repeat the process for the inside back cover.

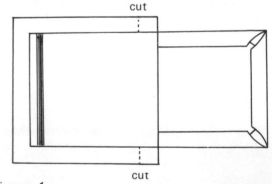

Diagram 1

Trim back the remaining fabric flaps at the top and bottom of the spine. To complete, glue the first page of the diary to the inside front cover, and the last page to the inside back cover, with craft glue.

70

Floral Design Lightshade

Materials Needed

- wire lightshade frame
- paper
- pencil
- scissors
- plain cotton fabric
- fusible webbing (cobweb)
- white organza
- assorted pressed flowers and leaves
- tweezers
- iron
- binding tape
- contact adhesive
- laces
- braids

To Make

Place the wire frame, on its side, on a piece of paper. Draw around the inside of one panel with a pencil, and cut out the pattern.

Lay the paper pattern on the cotton fabric, and cut out one piece of fabric for each panel, allowing an extra 2 cm around the edges. Cut a piece of fusible webbing and a piece of organza for each panel as well.

Place one panel of the cotton fabric on top of the paper pattern, as a guide, and arrange the

Illustration 1

pressed flowers and leaves on it. Use the tweezers to move the flowers around, until you are satisfied with the arrangement. Be careful to keep the arrangement in the centre of the panel (illustration 2).

Illustration 2

Lay first a panel of the fusible webbing, and then a panel of organza, on top of the flowers. Set the iron heat-control to 'Wool' and heat-set the three fabrics together.

Repeat this process for half the panels, matching the flowers in each panel. Leave the other half of the panels plain, simply fusing the cotton and organza together.

To bind the lightshade frame, measure the length of each wire strut and double it. Cut pieces of binding tape to this measurement. Glue each length of binding tape to the bottom ring at the base of each strut. Bind the tape around the wire strut, overlapping slightly and pulling tightly to prevent the tape from slipping. Finish by gluing the tape to the top ring. Repeat for each strut. Bind the top and bottom ring in the same manner.

Use the contact adhesive to attach the panels. Apply glue to the outside binding of one strut, position a plain fabric panel over this section of the frame, and rub until it has adhered. Repeat the process for every alternate plain section.

Return to the first panel glued, and glue the other side on to the frame, stretching it tightly. Repeat for the other panels. Stretch and glue the panels over the top and bottom rings in the same way. When all alternate panels are completed,

trim back all excess fabric with scissors (illustration 3).

Repeat the same process for the pressed-flower panels until the frame is completely covered. Decorate the lightshade with gathered lace and braid, covering all the raw edges on the struts and the top and bottom rings.

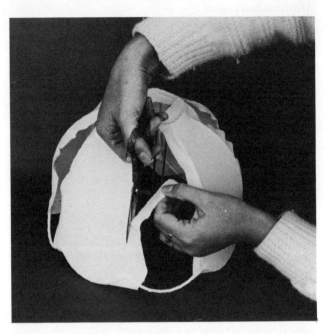

Illustration 3

Pressed-Flower Tissue-Box Cover

Materials Needed

   pencil
   thick white pasteboard
   Stanley knife
   scissors
   plain cotton fabric
   fusible webbing (cobweb)
   white organza
   assorted pressed flowers and leaves
   tweezers
   iron
   spray glue
   contact adhesive
   30 cm narrow gathered lace
   ruler
   1 metre of 6 cm wide gathered lace

To Make

Trace the paper pattern, transfer to the pasteboard, and cut out. The centre opening will also need to be cut out carefully, with a Stanley knife.

Cut out the plain cotton fabric to cover the pasteboard, allowing an extra 3 cm around the edges. Cut a piece of fusible webbing and a piece of organza to the same size. Lay the fabric exactly on top of the paper pattern as a guide, and arrange the pressed flowers and leaves on it. Use the tweezers to move the flowers around, until you are

Illustration 1

satisfied with the arrangement. Carefully lay first the fusible webbing, and then the organza, on top of the plain fabric. Set the iron heat-control to 'Wool' and heat-set the three fabrics together.

Spray-adhere the pasteboard to the plain side of the fabric. Pierce the cut-out centre of the fabric with the sharp point of the scissors, and cut the fabric into small strips (illustration 2).

Apply contact adhesive around the pasteboard side of the opening, pull the fabric over, and adhere. Trim back the fabric to neaten. Decorate around the inside of the opening with the narrow gathered lace, using contact adhesive.

Score four lines on the pasteboard, as shown on the pattern, using the point of the scissors and a ruler. Bend the four scored lines in to form a box shape. Glue the fabric on the two ends over on to the pasteboard (diagram 1).

Illustration 2

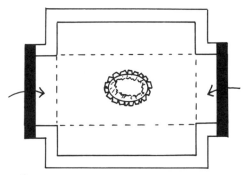

Diagram 1

Fold these two end pieces of pasteboard over, and adhere the fabric on either side of them on to the pasteboard sides of the box (illustration 3).

Apply contact adhesive to the L-shaped fabric in the corners of one side of the box and, when the glue is tacky, join the corners together and hold till dry. Repeat for the other side.

Glue the remaining loose fabric over to the inside of the box. Decorate around the outside of the tissue-box cover with the wide gathered lace.

Note: You can draft patterns for tissue boxes of any size by using the actual box.

Illustration 3

Pressed-Flower Picture Frame

Materials Needed

- pencil
- thick white pasteboard
- Stanley knife
- scissors
- plain cotton fabric
- fusible webbing (cobweb)
- white organza
- assorted pressed flowers and leaves
- tweezers
- iron
- polyester wadding
- spray glue
- contact adhesive
- 2.2 metres gathered lace
- 30 cm narrow ribbon
- picture or photograph

Illustration 1

To Make

Trace the paper patterns and transfer to the pasteboard, following the instructions given. Cut the two pieces needed, and carefully cut out the oval centre with the Stanley knife.

Cut the fabric into two rectangles, 3 cm larger

Illustration 2

all round than the pasteboard pieces. Cut one rectangle of the fusible webbing and one rectangle of the organza to the same size.

Lay one piece of the fabric exactly on top of the paper pattern as a guide, and arrange the pressed flowers and leaves on it. Use the tweezers to move the flowers around, until you are satisfied with the arrangement. Carefully lay first the fusible webbing, and then the organza, on top of the fabric. Set the iron heat-control to 'Wool' and heat-set the three fabrics together.

See the Lace Pot-Pourri Photograph Frame on page 32 for instructions on covering the two frame pieces.

Glue the gathered lace around the inside and outside edges with contact adhesive (illustration 2).

Make two small holes on the fabric side of the backing piece, in the positions shown on the pattern. Thread the narrow ribbon through the holes, and knot at the back.

Glue the picture or photograph into position on the pasteboard side of the backing piece. Glue the wrong sides of the two frame pieces together with contact adhesive.

Scented Floral Candles

Create sweet-smelling decorative candles by attaching pressed flowers and leaves to plain white candles. These candles are safe to light, and release a light and subtle perfume as they burn.

Materials Needed
    pressed flowers and leaves
    assorted plain white candles
    metal spoon
    paraffin wax
    saucepan
    scented oil

To Make
Position a flower on a candle, holding it in place with your finger. Heat the spoon in extremely hot

water, dry it, and press the spoon against the flower. As the wax softens, the flower will adhere to the candle.

Repeat this process, adding more flowers each time, until the design on the candle is complete.

Melt enough paraffin wax in the saucepan to cover the candle when it is held upright. Add a few drops of scented oil to the wax.

Holding the candle by the wick, carefully dip it into the melted wax for a few seconds, then hold it upright in the air to harden. When the candle has completely hardened it is ready for use.

Illustration 1

QUILLING

Quilling, or 'paper filigree' as it is often called, is a craft technique that involves rolling, gluing, and pinching 3 mm and 6 mm wide coloured paper into shapes, and then adhering them together to create a quilled design.

Quilling is used in a wide selection of giftware crafts (illustration 1), including decorative jewellery, gift cards, and wall plaque decorations.

This technique originated in fourteenth century England, where it was used to make substitute metal filigree in churches. The name 'quilling' came from the fact that the original works were rolled around a porcupine quill. Today a specially designed quilling tool is available, but a hat-pin or toothpick may be used instead. Precision-cut paper strips, which ensure evenness in your work, can readily be bought.

The technique of quilling is very simple to learn: you simply practise rolling the paper until you have achieved correct tension, so that, when released, the roll will give the desired effect.

Illustration 1

Basic Quilling

Materials Needed
   quilling paper
   quilling tool (hat-pin or toothpick)
   ruler
   scissors
   craft glue

To Make
Cut off the required length of quilling paper (as stated in the design pattern).

Hold the quilling tool in your right hand and, with the thumb and index finger of your left hand, press the end of the paper around the tool and begin rolling. As you roll the paper, keep the edges even and the roll very tight. Follow the directions opposite for each individual design.

Practise making each roll and scroll a few times to get used to the quilling tool, and to learn the size of shape to make from each length of paper. You will then be ready to show off your quilling talents by making beautiful arrangements such as the Quilled Floral Bouquet.

 Tight Roll: Roll a tight circle of paper, remove the tool, and glue the loose end.

 Loose Roll: Roll a tight circle of paper and remove the tool, allowing the roll to relax; glue the loose end.

 Teardrop: Make a loose roll, and pinch the glued end into a point with your fingers.

 Eye: Make a loose roll, and pinch both ends into points.

 Scroll: These are not glued, and may be rolled from one or both ends.

 Fringed Flower: Cut a length of paper along one side, roll into a tight roll, and glue the loose end. Carefully spread the cut side of the roll open.

Quilled Floral Bouquet

Quill this flowery arrangement from a rainbow of papers. Because the flowers and leaves are all made from basic quilling shapes, you will find that this lovely bouquet is far easier to make than you might expect.

Materials Needed

    waxed paper
    black marking pen
    pins
    corrugated cardboard
    scissors
    green paper
    ruler
    3 mm quilling paper in assorted colours, including green
    quilling tool (hat-pin or toothpick)
    craft glue
    toothpick
    6 mm quilling paper in 1 colour
    1 plain card

Illustration 1

To Make

Trace the Quilled Floral Bouquet pattern (diagram 7) on to the waxed paper with the black marking pen, and pin it to the cardboard.

Cut out five leaf shapes from the green paper, using diagram 1 as a guide. Glue these on to the waxed paper, in the positions shown on the pattern.

Diagram 1

For Flower 1, roll a 4 cm long tight roll with 3 mm green paper. Around this roll glue six 8 cm long coloured eyes (diagram 2). Make four of these flowers and glue them into position on the waxed

paper, using a toothpick to apply dots of glue to the pieces that touch.

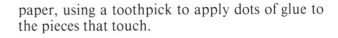

Diagram 2

For Flower 2, roll a 3 cm long tight roll for the centre of the flower. Around the centre glue five 6 cm long teardrops (diagram 3). Make four flowers, and glue them into position on the waxed paper.

Diagram 3

82

For a bud stem, make a 6 cm long green scroll, and glue 5 cm long coloured tight rolls to the sides (diagram 4). Make three bud stems, and glue them into position on the waxed paper.

Diagram 4

To make a stem of quilled leaves, roll 6 cm long green teardrops, and glue to a short length of green paper for the stem (diagram 5). Make three stems of leaves and glue them into position on the waxed paper.

Diagram 5

To make the ribbon bow, cut a 16 cm length of 6 mm quilling paper. Cut off a 1 cm piece from one end, and shape the rest into a bow (diagram 6). Glue the 1 cm piece over the centre of the bow to resemble the knot.

Diagram 6

For the streamers, cut two 5 cm lengths of the 6 mm quilling paper, trim inverted Vs into one end of each streamer, and glue uncut ends under the centre of the bow.

Glue five 5 cm lengths of 3 mm green paper, and adhere them under the bow for the bouquet stems.

To complete the bouquet, carefully transfer the leaves, flowers, stems, and bow to the front of the plain card. Illustration 1 gives a guide to positioning the quilled design. Use enough glue to make sure that the flowers adhere securely.

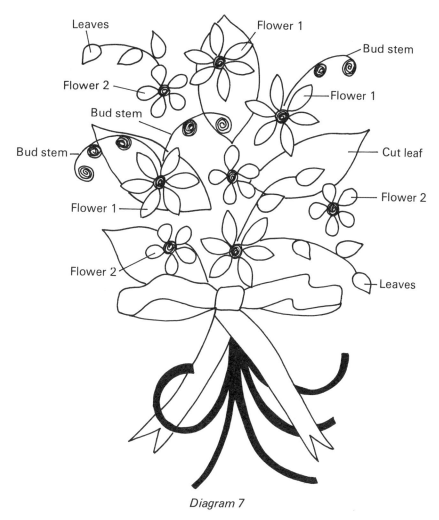

Diagram 7